The Saguaro Book

Merritt S. Keasey III

KENDALL/HUNT PUBLISHING COMPANY
Dubuque, Iowa, USA • Toronto, Ontario, Canada

Cover photo courtesy of E. Driscoll-Hunt

Copyright © 1981 by Kendall/Hunt Publishing Company

Library of Congress Catalog Card Number: 81-80188

ISBN 0-8403-2392-1

Printed in the United States of America

B   402392   01

Contents

Preface

The purpose of this book is to introduce the reader to an extremely unique plant—the saguaro cactus—and to the many plants and animals which share its Sonoran Desert habitat. Although many people may think of a desert as being a barren, desolate area, quite the opposite is true of the saguaro community, where life teems like no other place on earth. It is the author's hope that, through the reading of this book, more people will come to the realization that the desert is a complex and fragile environment which deserves all of the appreciation and protection we can give it.

I would like to take this opportunity to thank E. Driscoll-Hunt for the help she has given me in this project. Her spectacular sunset shot adorns the cover, and other examples of her fine photography are found throughout the book. I would also like to thank the members of the faculty of the University of Arizona who checked the original manuscript for accuracy, and the staff members—past and present— of the Arizona-Sonora Desert Museum, who contributed their ideas and editing comments. A very special thanks goes to William Panczner, my good friend and colleague, without whose support this book would not be possible, and to my dear wife, Lillian, who spent many long, tedious hours in the darkroom, processing photographs.

March 1981   Merritt S. Keasey III
                                              Tucson, Arizona

Introduction

The desert landscape of southern Arizona and northwestern Mexico is the home of the giant cactus known as the saguaro. Pronounced sa-WAHR-o and often spelled sahuaro, this name is derived from the Papago Indian's word for the plant. The saguaro's scientific name—*Carnegiea gigantea*—is in recognition of the Carnegie Institute of Washington, D.C., whose staff of Tucson's Desert Laboratory branch conducted many years of research on the saguaro cactus.

One of the largest cacti in the world, the saguaro is the most conspicuous plant of Arizona's desert land, and is widely used as a symbol of this region. For its protection, the National Park Service, in 1933, established the Saguaro National Monument on Tucson's far east side at the base of the Rincon Mountains. Within the boundaries of this 63,360 acre site is a forest made up mostly of large, aging plants whose numbers are rapidly becoming fewer. There are practically no young or seedling plants in the area. In the more recently opened Tucson Mountain Unit—15 miles west of the city—is a much more dense and younger stand of these giant cacti. In this stand many plants less than ten years old can be found.

The saguaro is found only in the Sonoran Desert region. (See Map on page 00.) It is limited to this range by a combination of several factors. On the northern and eastern edges it is limited primarily by temperature, for saguaros cannot survive in an area where the daytime temperature remains below the freezing point. The same factor also prohibits its growth at elevations much in excess of 4500 feet.

To the west, few saguaros occur beyond the Colorado River. There the limiting factor is the lack of rainfall. The opposite is probably the case, however, at the southern end of the saguaro's range. There, in the southern part of the Mexican state of Sonora, rainfall is higher, and the soil remains too moist for the proper growth of this desert plant. The few, scattered saguaros in that area are surrounded by many species of semi-tropical plants.

Saguaros are found on a few islands in the Gulf of California, and along the flat expanses of its northeastern coastline. Some are also found on the valley floors and in mountain canyons, but they occur in their greatest numbers on the south-facing slopes of rocky foothills. Not only are these the warmest areas, but they also meet the saguaros' need for well-drained soil.

To better understand the role of the saguaro in its environment, we must first understand its home, the Sonoran Desert. Bounded on the north by the rising mountains of central Arizona and on the east by Mexico's Sierra Madre, this vast desert extends southward through much of the state of Sonora, for which it was named. On the west it extends into southeastern California and southward into Baja, California. Its boundaries are not always easily distinguished, however, and therefore may not always be indicated in exactly the same position by scientists who map the region.

The Sonoran Desert is not one solid, continuous area, but is broken up—particularly on the eastern side—by a series of high mountain ranges whose plant and animal life differs from that of the desert floor. Toward the west these mountain ranges are smaller and lower and become completely desert habitat. It is in these low mountains, the valleys between them, and throughout the rocky foothills of the higher ranges that the saguaro forests grow.

The visitor center at Saguaro National Monument—Rincon Mt. Unit—on Tucson's east side.

The old, dwindling cactus forest in Saguaro National Monument's Rincon Mt. Unit.

The visitor center at Saguaro National Monument—Tucson Mt. Unit—on Tucson's west side.

The younger, more concentrated stand of saguaros in Saguaro National Monument's Tucson Mt. Unit.

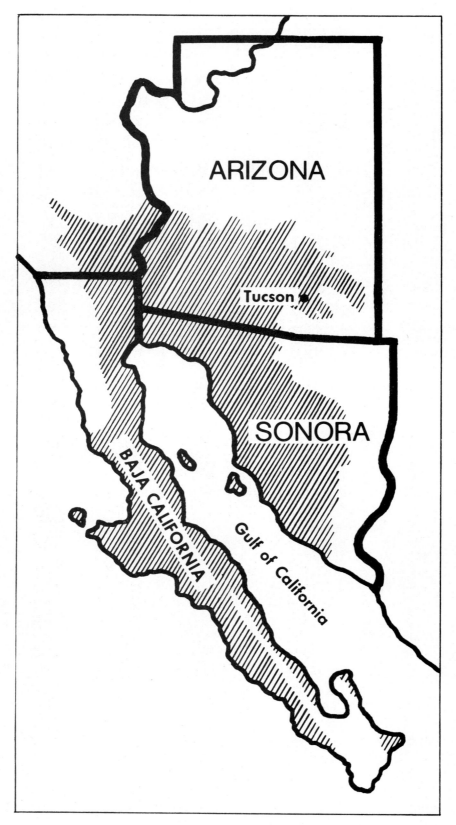

The Sonoran Desert—Saguaros are limited to the Arizona and Sonora portions of this desert.

The climate of the Sonoran Desert, although generally hot and dry, is one of extremes. Summer daytime temperatures often range well above 100° F., yet drop as much as 30 or more degrees at night. Winter temperatures are usually much lower, plunging beneath the freezing point on some nights. Again there is a large temperature differential between night and day, and the winter temperature may climb back to the 60s or 70s by mid-afternoon.

The annual rainfall varies from 12 inches in the eastern section, down to near zero in parts of the western portion. There are two rainy seasons, the greatest precipitation falling over most of the area during July, August, and September. During this period thunderstorms may occur almost daily, caused primarily by the flow of warm, moist air sweeping in from the Gulf of Mexico, and occasionally by tropical storms moving in from the southwest. Although covering only a small area, these storms are often violent and may be accompanied by strong winds, hail and intense lightning. Flashflooding is frequent. The farther west this moist air moves, the less moisture it contains. Therefore, the northwestern portion of the desert receives much less rainfall in the summer than do the southern and eastern sections.

The second rainy season occurs in the winter and is of a much more gentle nature. The rain falls slowly but steadily, soaking the ground and usually causing little runoff. These storms are more widespread, and are part of the large systems moving in from the Pacific Ocean.

Wherever temperature, soil and rainfall are all suitable for the saguaro's needs, the greatest numbers of these cacti are found. In some areas this may be for only a few acres, while elsewhere many square miles of desert mountains and foothills are covered by large stands of saguaros. In these cactus forests many different types of plants and animals live in close association with the saguaro. All are dependent one upon the other for their livelihood. It is the purpose of this book—through the use of illustrations and text—to help you to discover the importance of this close association of living things.

In the pages which follow you will be able to trace the entire life history of this remarkable cactus. It begins with the germination of a tiny seed within a shaded and protected area and continues through its growth to a giant which—after perhaps 175 years—may reach a height of over 40 feet and a weight of several tons. Its structure—both inside and out—will be examined, along with the production of flowers and fruit. You will learn about animals which prey upon the tiny saguaro seedlings, bore into the interior of the young plants, or feed upon its pollen and nectar, thereby carrying out the pollination necessary to its reproduction.

Periods of animal activity in the saguaro forest—both night and day—will be carefully examined. You will take a close look into the lives of such interesting creatures as the javelina, elf owl, and kangaroo rat, just to name a few. The saguaro has often been referred to as a "living apartment house", because of a number of species of birds nesting in the holes hollowed out within its towering arms and trunk by woodpeckers. The lives of these will also be discussed.

Although the saguaro dominates much of the desert landscape, there are many other plants living within the saguaro forest community, and some of these will be described. They range in size from the large palo verde, mesquite, and ironwood trees, to the tiny desert wildflowers which bloom briefly and quickly wither away. Other cacti which occur in the saguaro's range will also be examined. Some of them—such as the organ pipe and the night-blooming cereus—are closely related to the saguaro.

Man's relationship to the saguaro is the subject of another chapter. This describes the use of saguaro fruit as a food source, and its wooden ribs as a building material, by the Papago Indians. This chapter also points out modern man's destruction of the saguaro, not only in construction areas, but in our parks and monuments as well.

A book on the saguaro cactus would not be complete without a chapter devoted to its death, for even after it has been destroyed by wind, lightning, disease, vandalism, or other factors, this desert monarch continues to provide both food and shelter for many species of wildlife within its decaying carcass. Like the rest of this book, this chapter has been designed to further increase your knowledge and enjoyment of this fascinating plant, with the hope that with this knowledge will come appreciation and protection—not only of the saguaro, but of all living things.

Chapter 1

Seeds and Seedlings

A single seed of a saguaro is a tiny thing, no larger than a letter "o" of this print. Yet this small speck of material has the ability to sprout into a cactus which may eventually reach a height of over forty feet and a weight of several tons. Before it can begin growth as a seedling, a saguaro seed must survive. There are many things which can happen to a seed before it has a chance to germinate. Of the many thousands of seeds produced each year by one giant cactus, scientists estimate that only one out of every 1,000 will germinate. Many of these seedlings will quickly die and only a very small percentage continue to live and grow, even for a short time. During its lifetime an average saguaro may produce millions of seeds, yet perhaps only one of these may ever become a mature plant. In the following paragraphs we will see why this is so.

As soon as the ripe saguaro fruits begin to split open, the contents of many are quickly eaten. The red, juicy pulp and the seeds within it are a welcome supply of food and moisture for many creatures. The birds are the first to get to the fruit while it still clings to the saguaro, high above the ground. Even birds such as the flycatchers that otherwise feed only upon insects come to dine upon the ripe saguaro fruit. In some areas of the saguaro forest the fruit is harvested by Papago Indians, who use it for many purposes.

Much of the fruit which falls to the ground is eaten by animals which cannot reach it while it is still on the plant. Even such tiny creatures as the harvester ants carry many seeds off to their underground burrows, storing them there for future use. Unless the seed is actually crushed or digested, being eaten does not necessarily mean that it is destroyed. If swallowed whole, a saguaro seed may pass through the digestive tract of an animal completely unharmed. But whether eaten or not, many seeds will end up in a location where germination can never take place. Some fall onto bare ground where they perish from lack of moisture and excessive heat. Others become buried too deeply to germinate.

A saguaro seed needs several things before it can sprout. It must receive the right amount of moisture, the proper temperature, and adequate light. Some saguaro seeds may lie dormant for as long as three years, but whenever these conditions are correct, growth begins within the seed, usually within 48 hours. If it has sprouted from a seed which was buried at approximately one-eighth of an inch below the surface it will have the best chance for continued growth. Here it receives the proper combination of light and protection. If deeper or shallower, it may die.

There are many things which can quickly cause the destruction of a seedling saguaro. A small animal may eat it, or a larger one step upon it. A heavy rainstorm may wash it away, or the lack of rain over a long period may cause it to dry up. Temperatures below freezing for too long a period of time also will destroy it.

Approximately 2,000 of these tiny black seeds are produced by each saguaro fruit.

These tiny seedlings are four months old.

These seedling saguaros are fifteen months old.

Saguaro seedlings which start to grow out on the open desert floor, exposed to the full rays of the sun, will soon perish. The only ones with any chance of survival are those which begin their growth in the protective shelter of a plant or a rock. Often one or more young saguaros may be found growing beneath the overhanging branches of a mesquite, ironwood, palo verde or bursage. These trees and shrubs are referred to as "nurse plants," for they provide shade and protection. Smaller plants, which are also using the nurse plant for shelter, provide further cover, and help to hold the soil together, preventing the tiny seedlings from being washed away.

Rabbits, ground squirrels, woodrats and cactus mice all eat young cacti, and it is only the best protected seedlings which escape detection by these small mammals. No matter how well hidden, however, many small saguaros are destroyed by larvae of the cactus weevil. The female beetle lays a single egg in the skin of a small saguaro. Upon hatching the larva burrows into the soft interior and begins to feed. Within a few weeks there is nothing left but a hollow shell. The larva pupates, later hatching into an adult weevil. Only the very small plants—usually less than two inches in height—are destroyed.

This small saguaro, perhaps as much as ten years old,
germinated within the protection of this bursage.

A cactus weevil looks for a place to deposit her eggs
on this young saguaro.

The cactus weevil is much more commonly found feeding upon the prickly pear cactus, and no one knows how many young saguaros may be eaten. A study by the University of Arizona and the U.S. Department of Agriculture of transplanted saguaro seedlings revealed that up to thirteen percent were destroyed by the larvae of this insect in some of the test plots. Later studies show that the larvae of the longhorned cactus beetle also feed upon young saguaros.

A saguaro seedling grows very slowly. A young plant may take as long as five years to reach the height of one inch. This does not mean, however, that it will be only two inches tall at the end of ten years, for the growth rate has been increasing since its germination. Since this growth is mostly dependent upon temperature and moisture conditions, there will be a variation in the growth of saguaros in different locations, as well as from year to year.

The tip of a young saguaro continues to grow upward year after year. It will, however, remain a single stem for many years—even long after it has begun to bear fruit. The development of arms will come much later. At the height of approximately eight feet the first flower buds appear around its crown. Forty-five to 55 years have then passed since the little seedling first broke through the ground. The nurse plant which gave it shelter may already have died, but the saguaro no longer needs its protection. It has now become a mature plant, capable of producing seeds.

These potted seedlings have reached a height of over an inch in just three years and three months, due to the extra care and protection of their indoor environment.

Chapter 2

Growth and Anatomy

By the time a saguaro reaches eight feet in height it begins to produce seed. In the late spring, flowers appear upon the crown of the young plant's single stem. These flowers develop into the seed-laden fruit. At this size the plant's growth rate is slowing down, and it may take four years or more to gain a foot in height. Somewhere around the age of 75 to 100 years and a height of 12 to 20 feet, arm buds appear. This usually occurs at the thickest part of the saguaro's trunk, approximately eight feet above the ground, which was also the height where the first flowers began to develop. Within a few years the upcurving arms also begin to produce flowers and fruit.

The arms of a saguaro usually grow at the same rate as the main stem, although some grow faster or slower, depending upon varying conditions. They normally extend upwards, but exceptionally long arms may twist down, due to their weight. Occasionally they may touch the ground and curve upwards again, giving the cactus an unusual appearance. They do not normally take root, however, as do the stems of some cacti.

This arm bud has just emerged from the side of the cactus and will be this plant's first arm.

**The arms on this cactus have all curled downwards,
giving it an unusual appearance.**

Once they have produced arms, no two saguaros look exactly alike. While one may grow straight and erect, others may be bent and twisted. Some may have only two or three arms, while others may have 10, 20, or even as many as 50. Now and then small arms will branch from another arm. This usually happens when the original arm tip has been damaged. This is also true of the growing tip of the main stem. Several new branches will often appear around the damaged tip. Larger and older specimens of saguaros often grow more arms high above the first set, while the larger arms may also produce branches.

The outside of a saguaro consists of a tough layer of tissue which is covered with a waxy coating which helps to prevent the escape of moisture. Beneath this first layer is another layer, made up of the chlorophyll containing cells, and it is within these cells that photosynthesis takes place. This is the process of carbohydrate production which all green plants perform and without which life could not exist.

The large arms on this saguaro have produced
smaller arms, and even many of them have yet still
more arm buds. Another interesting fact is that this
plant does not produce flowers.

Surrounded by these outer layers, most of the interior of the saguaro is made up of thin-walled
water storage cells. Following a rain, the saguaro's roots absorb moisture, which is transported up into
the plant's interior and stored in these cells. The strong, flexible outer covering of the cactus is arranged
in pleats or folds, much like the sides of an accordion. When water is gained or lost, the accordion-like
structure allows the stem to expand or contract. Over a long period of time without rainfall a saguaro
may lose a considerable amount of its girth, but gain it back again during the next rainy season. As
much as a 16 inch difference in circumference has been recorded. One may hear of instances where
saguaros have taken in so much water that they have split their sides, but this seldom happens, and is
probably due to already weakened tissues.

Because of its great amount of water storage, a large saguaro may weigh several tons. Supporting
the massive weight of the water-storing tissues is a stout inner skeleton. This consists of a circular column
of wood ribs—usually 13 to 20—which runs up the center of the main stem and branches out into each
arm. The water storage cells entirely encompass this wooden column, both within its center and around
its outside. It is within the outer cells of these ribs that the water and nutrients are transported.

A cutaway section of the expandable, accordion-like structure of a saguaro cactus. Notice the supporting ribs in the center of the trunk. (Drawing by Gary J. Dixon.)

On the edge of each outer fold of the saguaro's exterior is a row of small protrusions known as areoles. These are spaced about one inch apart and from each grows a group of spines. The saguaro's spines actually serve very little as protection, and it is believed that their most important function is providing shade. This may at first seem impossible, for how could such thin objects as cactus spines possibly shade such a large plant? But if we are to look closely at a saguaro—particularly the smaller ones—on a sunny day, we shall quickly see that the large groupings of spines do, indeed, cast a great deal of shade upon the saguaro's outer surface.

A large saguaro usually does not have many spines along the lower portion of its trunk, these having gradually decayed or been worn off through the years. Once these lower spines are lost, they do not grow back again, but this portion of an older plant is hardened and calloused into a bark-like material and does not need nearly as much shade or protection as the tender, growing tip.

Because of its large mass, the interior of a saguaro maintains a much more stable temperature than that of its surroundings. During the heat of a summer day this interior is considerably cooler than the air temperature, for it would take much longer than one day to heat up the bulk of a large cactus. On cool nights the reverse is true, for the cactus retains some of the heat stored within it during the day, and the interior is therefore warmer than the outside temperature. These conditions make the inside of a large cactus an ideal place for many creatures to build their homes, and an entire chapter of this book is devoted to that subject.

A close-up of the interwoven latticework of each spine bearing areole.

As a saguaro grows, the lower spines fall off and the trunk hardens into a bark-like material.

A shallow, widespread root system supports the towering structure of the saguaro
cactus. (Drawing by Gary J. Dixon.)

The roots of a saguaro are shallow, and extend outwards in all directions. They are approximately equal in length to the height of the plant. With this arrangement they not only give support to the towering frame, but are also able to take advantage of even a slight amount of rainfall. There are a few roots which extend a short ways downwards, but there is not a long taproot like that of many plants.

Occasionally a saguaro may grow in a strange manner. The tip of the growing stem will spread outwards into a large fan, several times the width of the main trunk. A plant which grows in this fashion is referred to as cristate or crested. The cause of this strange formation is not fully understood. Cristate saguaros are not very common, but at least one specimen can usually be found within any large stand of saguaros. In spite of their strange shape, cristates are able to produce flowers and fruit in the same manner as a normal plant.

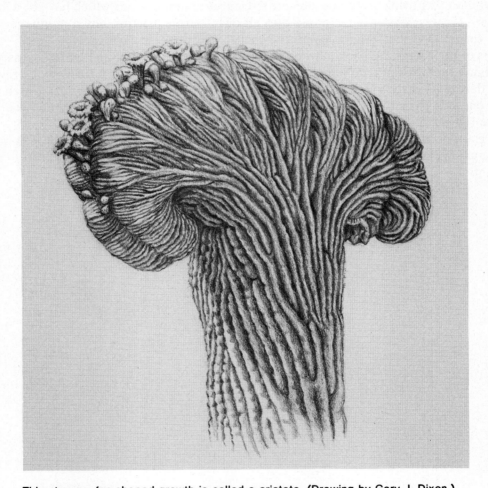

This strange, fan-shaped growth is called a cristate. (Drawing by Gary J. Dixon.)

Many of the larger specimens of saguaros which we see as we pass along a roadway through a saguaro forest are at least 150 years old. In order to better understand just how old this really is, let's take a look at a single specimen of this age. When it was a seedling, the city of Tucson, Arizona, was a small, dusty Spanish settlement, surrounded by a large adobe wall to protect it from raiding bands of Apaches. By the time the cactus had reached the height of a man, President Abraham Lincoln had signed a bill declaring this part of the country to be Arizona Territory. Arms were beginning to appear upon its sides when Arizona finally received statehood in 1912.

During its century and a half of existence, this individual saguaro—like all of the others around it—has been a very important part of the community of plants and animals which have lived with it. Each summer it has provided fruit pulp and seeds for a multitude of hungry creatures. The holes within the upper portions of its trunk and arms indicate entrances to nest cavities which have been hollowed out by woodpeckers. Generations of these, along with elf owls, purple martins, and a number of other desert birds have in turn reared their young within the cool shelter of these cavities.

The sides of the cactus are pock-marked and scarred by the chewing and boring of insects, rodents, and other animals, and by the scraping of the wind-blown limbs of the nurse tree which provided shelter for the plant during its early life. The upper half of one arm has been broken off by a high wind, and a large scar on one side of its trunk indicates the wound left some years ago by a thoughtless human who decided to use the cactus as a target for his stone throwing.

But the giant cactus still stands. In the following chapters we shall take a closer look at what takes place in the saguaro community, including the circumstances which will eventually lead to the death of the aging plant.

Chapter 3

Flowers and Fruit

As early as mid-April, groups of flower buds begin to appear around the tips of the trunk and stems of mature saguaros. Each bud grows from a spine-bearing areole. At times these buds may appear well down the stem or arm, and upon rare occasions one or more may sprout from the main trunk only a few feet above the ground. Usually by the first of May, the white, waxy-petaled blossoms begin to open. This blossom has been chosen by Arizona as its state flower.

Saguaro flowers are night-blooming, beginning to open just after sundown and becoming fully opened by midnight. Unlike many other night-blooming cacti whose flowers close soon after sunrise, the saguaro blossoms remain open during much of the next day. They usually close by mid-afternoon and do not open again. It is during this period of less than 24 hours that pollination must take place. The large, white blooms attract night-flying creatures, particularly the nectar bats and many types of moths. These flit rapidly from one flower to another, taking up the nectar contained within them. In doing so, they spread the pollen from one saguaro flower to another.

Flower buds circle the crown of a low hanging saguaro limb.

The early morning light touches a group of newly-opened
saguaro blossoms. By late afternoon they will close,
and the fruiting bodies will begin to develop.

Arizona's state flower, the saguaro blossom.

A bat circles a group of saguaro blossoms.

As the moth or bat thrusts its head down into the open flower, it brushes against the circle of pollen-bearing stamens, which make up the male part of the flower. The pollen sticks to the animal's body and is then transferred in the same manner to the pistil of another flower, which is the single, central, female part of the blossom. It is interesting to note that fruit will not develop from a saguaro flower pollinated with its own pollen, or even with pollen from a flower of the same arm. Rarely a few fruit will set from the cross-pollination between flowers on different arms of the same plant. In order to be at all successful, the pollen must be carried from the flower of one saguaro to that of another.

In the daylight hours, a number of other creatures begin to feed upon the sweet nectar, thereby continuing the pollination. Ants, wasps, bees, and butterflies are among the insects which visit the flowers. Many birds also come. The largest and most notable of these are the white-winged doves. There are also birds which feed upon the insects attracted by the nectar.

The blossoming period of the saguaro usually continues throughout the month of June. (A few saguaro flowers may be seen blooming here and there during almost every month of the year, but these are few and far between.) Not all of the blossoms which open upon the saguaro will produce fruit. Some will not be successfully pollinated. Others will be knocked off by wind or rain, or by the birds which light upon them. There is a species of moth which lays its eggs within the base of the flower. The larvae of this moth eat the fruiting tissue, ending its chances to produce ripe fruit. Buds which appear on low-hanging arms have much less chance to survive than those higher up, for small animals are often able to reach them.

Most of the fruit ripen in June. The flower heads have shriveled and the fruit swell and ripen until they split open, exposing the red interior. From the time that a flower opens to the time that the fruit splits is a period of about one month. Birds and flying insects are usually the first to discover this new food source, and descend upon the saguaros in large numbers. Doves, orioles, woodpeckers, thrashers, and cactus wrens are among the numerous creatures which feed upon the seeds and pulp of the saguaro fruit. Most of these birds nest within the saguaro community, some within the giant cactus itself, although a few may come in from nearby areas.

The fruit ripens under the hot desert sun, splitting open to reveal the red pulp and black seeds.

A curvebilled thrasher feeds on the juicy pulp and seeds of a fallen saguaro fruit.

Flies, bees, wasps, beetles, butterflies, and moths swarm over the pulp, feeding upon its sweet juice. Ants also find the source of nourishment quickly, climbing up the saguaro's tall trunk to join the feast. Indians also arrive as soon as the fruit ripens. Knocking the fruit from the cactus with long poles, they gather it into baskets and carry it back to their camp where it is prepared for future consumption.

As the fruit falls to the ground the seeds and pulp are quickly consumed by animals which have been unable to reach the fruit while they are still on the plant. Quail, ants, ground-dwelling beetles, and many other small creatures are quickly attracted to it. Coyotes and foxes, skunks, javelina and badgers are among the larger mammals which make use of the fallen fruit as a portion of their diet. Rodents of many kinds also take advantage of this readily available food source. During the daytime the Harris antelope squirrels, roundtailed ground squirrels, and rock squirrels reap the harvest, while at night, packrats, pocket mice, cactus mice, kangaroo rats, and other nocturnal rodents compete with the other creatures for any newly-fallen fruit.

This little Harris ground squirrel enjoys prickly pear fruit also.

Each fruit contains an average of 2,000 seeds. As many as 30 fruit may be produced upon a single stem or arm. Considering an average saguaro to have three arms plus a main stem, we find that a plant of this size is capable of producing up to 240,000 seeds per year. Since a saguaro evidently never becomes too old to bear fruit, its seed production may last for over 100 years. Consider, therefore, that the total amount of seeds produced over this period of time would number in the millions. Consider also the fact that it would be necessary for only one of these millions of seeds to germinate and grow to maturity in order to maintain the saguaro's population balance.

In a stand of 10 saguaros per acre, there may be as many as 2.4 million seeds produced per acre each year. In a thick stand of from 25 to 30 plants per acre there could be three times that many seeds. Again, however, we must remember that only a small percentage of seeds produced each year will germinate, and few—if any—of these seedlings will survive to maturity.

The fruiting period usually ends around mid-July. Up to this time it has been very hot and dry. Now the summer rainy season comes, and the strong winds and heavy rainfall often knock off the few fruit still remaining on the stems. Those animals which have been feeding upon the pulp and seeds of the giant cacti's fruit must look elsewhere for food. But there are many other food sources in the saguaro community—a fact which we shall learn more about in the following chapters.

Chapter 4

A Living Apartment House

During its long life, an individual saguaro may become the home of many different creatures. Even before the plant grows arms, a Gila woodpecker or a gilded flicker may excavate nest cavities into its trunk high above the ground. The plant tissues then harden around the hollowed-out areas, and it is within the protection of these cavities that the woodpeckers raise their young, safe from most predators. These hardened forms, commonly referred to as "saguaro shoes", often are found within the debris of a fallen and decayed saguaro.

When the woodpeckers have abandoned the hole, other birds use it to raise their families. Purple martins and flycatchers are among them, along with the ever-present house sparrow (English sparrow) and the starling—both introduced species. At times a large saguaro may contain several active nests with two or more species of birds present. In residential areas, particularly where there are bird feeding stations, saguaros may tend to have more holes and a larger population of birds in them. This is due to the increased food supply which enables the birds to successfully raise more young.

A saguaro shoe—the calloused tissue formed around the hollowed-out nesting site within the saguaro.

A gila woodpecker surveys the landscape from a hole which it has drilled into the saguaro's interior.

Several of the desert's smaller predatory birds make use of the saguaro nest cavities. One of these is the American kestrel (sparrow hawk), a small falcon which, despite its name, preys more upon insects than it does upon anything else. Another is the tiny elf owl, a bird which stands only 135mm to 160mm high (5.3 to 6.3 inches). Emerging at night, this little owl searches the saguaro community for insects, spiders, centipedes and scorpions, carrying them back to its nest where two or three hungry owlets await its return. A larger owl of the saguaro community, and one that is predatory upon the small rodents of the area, is the screech owl. About twice the size of an elf owl, this nocturnal bird may also make its home in the saguaro cavities.

Not all birds which build their nests in saguaros use the hollowed-out cavities, however. Mourning doves and white-winged doves sometimes construct their flimsy, stick platforms where the saguaro arms join the trunk. The cactus wren may also weave its enclosed grass nest there or make use of an abandoned woodpecker hole, but this is quite uncommon. The wren much prefers the more protective confines of the smaller, but more spiny, cholla cactus.

Many larger birds also choose the cradle formed by two or more upward curving saguaro arms as a nesting site. Among these are redtailed hawks, Harris hawks, great horned owls and ravens. Along the northern shores of the Gulf of California, and on a few of its islands, ospreys, great blue herons, and night herons also nest on the saguaros and other large cacti.

The
saguaro
community.

Photo by E. Driscoll-Hunt

Saguaros and
palo verde trees
in bloom.

Photo by E. Driscoll-Hunt

A rare scene—
snow in the desert.

Flower buds
begin to appear.

The
first blossom
opens.

Each day,
more flowers
bloom.

The flower heads
have shriveled
and fruit begins
to swell.

The fruit ripens
and splits open,
revealing red,
juicy interior.

Fruit begins
to fall
from plant.

Goldpoppies cover the hillside
at Picacho Peak.

An ocotillo blooms with
brilliant red tassels.

An ironwood tree in full bloom.

The hedgehog
cactus' blossoms
are among the largest
and most colorful
in the desert.

Large,
yellow blossoms
adorn this
prickly pear plant.

This tiny
pincushion cactus is
very inconspicuous
when it is
not in bloom.

The brittlebush
is a common plant
in the saguaro
community.

A night-blooming plant
like the saguaro,
the sacred datura
is a relative
of the tomato.

The large,
brilliant red flower
of the coral bean
is one of the
most spectacular
in the desert.

The mariposa lily is one of the most colorful of the spring flowers.

The globe mallow is a common spring flower in the desert.

The Parry penstemon is a favorite of the hummingbirds.

A desert tortoise
munches grass
among the wildflowers.

The Gila monster
is Arizona's only
venomous lizard.

The
western diamondback—
one of the most
formidable denizens
of the saguaro
community.

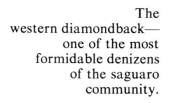

Screech owls are among the many birds which make use of the holes the woodpeckers have hollowed out. (Photo by E. Driscoll-Hunt.)

This mourning dove has constructed her nest in the crotch of two saguaro arms. Here she will raise two or three broods of young.

Although usually prefering the more protective confines of a jumping cholla, this cactus wren has constructed its woven grass nest within the deep crotch of a saguaro.

Birds are not the only animals which occur within nest cavities of a large saguaro, for many small creatures also use them for a place to find food or refuge. Bats are the only mammal which commonly use these cavities but many types of insects and arachnids do. Among these are katydids, grasshoppers, flies, gnats, mosquitos, bedbugs, moths and bees. Wasps build their paper-like nests within them. Carrion beetles feed upon droppings and other animal remains, while other types of beetles use the hole only as a resting site. Bird mites are common, being parasitic upon the feathered occupants. Spiders also are plentiful, feeding upon many of the insects. One of the most common inhabitants is the springtail, a primitive insect with a springlike appendage on its abdomen which enables it to leap about like a grasshopper.

Although most predators are unable to reach the nest holes in the saguaro's trunk or arms, there are a few which can. Snakes—particularly the agile racers—are able to reach them by winding their way up the trunk, although not without some difficulty. Nest holes in a saguaro growing within a large tree or shrub are particularly vulnerable, for the tree limbs offer a convenient passageway to the cactus' upper extremities.

A snake's approach to a nest which contains eggs or young birds often causes a great deal of commotion among the local bird population. The cactus wrens in particular join together in a scolding chorus, while the thrashers will attack the snake, hitting it with their feet as they dive by. The noise and bombardment does little to discourage the intruder, however, and the eggs or nestlings often are consumed. But baby birds are not the only things which the snake eats, for mice, lizards and other snakes—even small rattlesnakes—are included in the racer's diet.

Nor is the snake's role in the saguaro forest just that of a predator, for it may itself become a meal for a larger creature. Redtailed hawks, one of the largest predatory birds of the area, are prevalent, circling silently overhead in search of prey. Should a racer cross an open stretch of ground where one of these birds hunts, it will be quickly snatched up in the hawk's strong talons and carried back to the nest, to be divided among several hungry young hawks.

There are even a few creatures which feed upon the living tissues of the saguaro cacti. Among these are beetle larvae and the larvae of the cactobrosis moth. This moth is believed to be one of the carriers of the bacteria which sometimes destroys the giant cactus. (See Chapter Eight, The Death of a Saguaro.)

Even around the spreading root structure of a living saguaro we find a wide variety of wildlife. Within the 80 foot diameter which a large saguaro's root system may cover, there are a number of rodent burrows, some active, others perhaps unused. Smaller holes have been dug by spiders, insects, and other tiny creatures. Beneath the surface, insect larvae feed upon rootlets of the saguaro and other plants. One of the most notable of these is the cicada, a large insect related to the tiny aphids, and often miscalled "locust."

Cicada nymphs spend several years underground, feeding upon root sap. In the late spring or early summer they come up out of the ground, the back of the nymph's outer skeleton splits open, and the adult insect emerges. Numbers of these discarded shells are often found clinging to the lower trunks of saguaros during this time, and the buzzing song of the male cicada is heard throughout the saguaro forest.

The animals which we have discussed in this chapter are some of those which live in or upon the giant cactus. There are many other creatures which live within the saguaro community. Some feed upon the animals which make the saguaro their home. Others are eaten by them. Each is dependent in many ways upon all of the plants and animals of this habitat. This close relationship of plant and animal, and of predator and prey, will be further examined in the next chapter, A Day and a Night in the Saguaro Forest.

The loud buzzing of the male cicadas is a common sound in the saguaro forest during the early summer months.

Chapter 5

A Day
and a Night
in the Saguaro Forest

If you were to visit a saguaro forest on a hot summer's day, you might think that very few animals lived there. During the daytime, particularly in the hotter part of the year, most of the desert animals remain in hiding. Those that are active spend much of their time in the shade, and when necessary, hurry quickly across open spaces. Whiptailed lizards scratch about among the piles of seed pods scattered beneath a palo verde tree, searching for insects. Birds flit back and forth, alternately resting and feeding within the shade and shelter of the larger plants. High overhead a turkey vulture circles, keeping a close watch upon the ground beneath for a dead or dying animal.

The shrill buzzing of the male cicadas and the occasional rustling of a foraging lizard or bird are perhaps the only sounds to be heard. Now and then a gust of wind makes a soft sighing through the spines of the giant cacti. Suddenly a low roar of rushing wind calls our attention to a dust devil churning its way across the desert floor. Resembling a miniature tornado, this whirling funnel has been set in motion by hot air rising from the ground. Usually only kicking up some dust and a few leaves, most dust devils cause little damage, although larger ones have been known to damage saguaros.

A jackrabbit sits quietly beneath a mesquite tree, its huge ears partly erect. One might think that it was listening intently to some far-off sound, but actually it is only doing what all of the other desert animals are doing—keeping cool. The rabbit's ears are acting as cooling mechanisms, the blood flowing through the many blood vessels being cooled as the heat is radiated from them. The rabbit sits with the surface of its ears oriented towards a certain area of the north sky, which—surprisingly enough—is just a little bit cooler than the rest of the animal's surroundings. As the heat radiates outwards, the rabbit's body is cooled.

As the sun sinks lower in the late afternoon, the desert begins to lose some of its heat, and the creatures begin to emerge from their daytime refuges. The ground squirrels come up from burrows and forage about in search of seeds and other food. Lizards increase their search for insects, and snakes prowl about, seeking both the squirrels and lizards. A number of birds also increase their activity, and their calls are heard throughout the saguaro forest. But this period of afternoon activity is short, for soon the sun sets and the daytime animals once again retire to their hiding places.

Shortly after sundown a lone coyote crawls from beneath the low hanging branches of a palo verde tree where it has spent the day. Stretching once or twice, it lifts its muzzle to the sky and gives the yipping cry for which it is so well known. After several calls it is answered from a short distance away, and the lone animal is soon joined by another. The pair then heads off in search of food. During their hunt they may come across the resting place of the jackrabbit, and a wild chase begins. Sometimes a chase of this nature ends up with a jackrabbit meal for the coyotes, but often the speedy creature escapes and the coyotes have to look elsewhere. They may next attempt to catch a packrat or a cactus mouse. When available, however, a stomach full of saguaro fruit is much preferred and more easily obtained.

Turkey vultures are a common bird in the saguaro community.

A black-tailed jackrabbit stands poised to run. The long ears of this big hare act as cooling mechanisms during the hot summer.

The coyote spends the hot daytime hours sleeping in the shade of a mesquite tree.

The coyotes are not alone in this nightly hunt for food, for many other creatures are now beginning to move in the coolness of the night. A bobcat emerges from a rock crevice high up on a hillside and silently makes its way down to the desert floor. A cottontail feeding upon a patch of desert grass may become its prey, or with a quick pounce it may capture a mourning dove roosting on a low branch of an ironwood tree.

A small herd of javelina clatters down a rocky wash, grunting to each other. Often called "wild pig," this hoofed animal is actually not very closely related to domestic pigs. Many stories are told of the ferociousness of these creatures, but most are quite exaggerated. While it is true that they will sometimes defend themselves with their long, sharp tusks, they usually turn and run at the least sign of danger. Their food is varied, consisting of roots, cactus pads and fruit, and other desert vegetation.

The gray fox is a shy, usually silent predator which will often climb into trees in search of lizards or bird nests. It also is fond of fruit and berries. A smaller member of the canine family, the kit fox, stays on the ground in its search for food, and often dines upon the little Merriam's kangaroo rat which is quite common in the area, particularly in the lower, sandier deserts.

The kangaroo rat digs its tunnels among the roots of a creosote bush or other small shrub, mounding the dirt up around its lower branches. This small rodent is well-known for its ability to go throughout its life without ever drinking water. Feeding only upon dry seeds, its water needs are met by the small amount of moisture which it metabolizes from them. To conserve this moisture, the kangaroo rat lives in a burrow beneath the surface where it is relatively cool and moist, and comes to the surface only at night when the temperatures are lower and the humidity higher. Its highly efficient kidneys also reduce the water lost from the body by concentrating the urine to a paste. A unique area in its nasal passages extracts much of the moisture from the air which it exhales. One of many different types of desert rodents, the kangaroo rat is prey, not only for the foxes, but for snakes, owls and many other predators as well.

Bristles raised and large tusks showing, this javelina
warns off the intruder.

The kangaroo rat is a common rodent in the low desert areas.

The wildlife that is active during a desert night is widely varied. Skunks, owls, snakes—both venomous and non-venomous—and many other animals exist in the saguaro community, feeding upon plants and animals and being fed upon in turn. Among these is the Gila monster, the only venomous lizard in the United States. Feeding upon bird eggs, small rodents and lizards, this large lizard prowls about in the evening hours during much of the year.

Tinier creatures which are seldom seen during the daytime also emerge to hunt. Scorpions and centipedes crawl from beneath rocks and dead saguaros in search of insects. Tarantulas, wolf-spiders and trap-door spiders all come out of their underground homes and search about for prey, or wait at their burrow's entrance for an insect or other edible creature to come by.

Dawn brings a new flurry of activity to the saguaro community. By the time the sun has risen, the nocturnal animals have returned to their homes. Many birds are especially active, for the coolness of the early morning hours is their time of day. A covey of Gambel's quail wanders about, feeding upon seeds. A pyrrhuloxia sings from its perch high up on a saguaro top. A roadrunner chases a small rodent in and out among the bushes.

The large tarantula, although formidable looking, is quite harmless. (Photo by E. Driscoll-Hunt.)

The roadrunner, a member of the cuckoo family, feeds upon lizards, snakes and other small desert animals.

Some larger creatures are also active. A few mule deer browse peacefully along an arroyo bank, while nearby a badger enlarges its burrow in the desert floor. As the sun climbs higher, the temperature soars, and animal activity once again slows down.

Day after day this cycle is repeated throughout the saguaro forest, each plant and each animal playing an important role in the community. Each day new life begins and each day some life ends. Ground squirrels are born. Quail hatch. Saguaro seeds germinate. Some of the young squirrels will be eaten—by hawks, by snakes, by roadrunners. Others will die from accident or disease. But a few will survive. The brood of newly-hatched quail will shrink in number day by day, individuals being preyed upon, or separated from the covey. Again, some will live to carry on the species. As we have learned, most of the saguaro seedlings will not survive, but a few will continue to grow. In the meantime, older plants will die, uprooted by strong winds, struck by lightning, or destroyed by other factors. Both day and night, life and death are a natural part of the saguaro community.

Mule deer are the largest inhabitants of the saguaro forest.

Chapter 6

Other Plants
of the
Saguaro Community

Although the saguaro, due to its large size, dominates the scene, many other plants live in close association with it. From the tiniest of wildflowers to the largest of the desert trees, each serves a valuable function in this community, providing both food and shelter for many living things.

Among the largest and most common of these plants is the foothill palo verde, a tree which may grow to a height of 25 feet. The palo verde, whose Spanish name means "green tree", is so called because of its entirely green bark. Even the trunk and larger limbs, usually brown or grayish on other trees, are of a green hue. The foothill palo verde serves as "nurse plant", not only for young saguaros, but for other types of cacti and other plants as well. In the spring its yellow blossoms are a source of pollen for insects, and later in the summer its beans are eaten by many creatures.

Another common tree in this area is the mesquite. It also produces large quantities of flowers and edible beans, and provides shade for many species of plants and animals. Its hard wood has long been used by mankind for firewood and for construction, and because of this, many of the older, larger specimens of mesquite trees have been removed from the desert.

The ocotillo is a plant often mistakenly called a cactus. Although it bears long, sharp spines, it is not a cactus. Its only close relative is the boojum, or cirio, of Baja, California and Sonora, Mexico. During dry or cold periods of the year, the ocotillo loses all of its leaves and looks like a cluster of spiny, gray sticks. The loss of leaves conserves moisture. With warmth and moisture, green leaves once again sprout from each stem. Whether in leaf or not, each spring the ocotillo blooms, its spikes of orange-red blossoms vividly contrasting with the usual greens and browns of the desert around it.

The limberbush is a plant which only has leaves during the summer rains. Usually not more than three feet high, this shrub is hardly noticeable among the other desert vegetation during most of the year, but when in full leaf, the shiny, green, heart-shaped leaves stand out prominently. The roots and stems contain a red pigment used as a dye by Indians. Because of this red coloration, the Spanish name for this plant, sangre de drago, means, "blood of the dragon."

The fairy duster is a small shrub related to the mesquite and palo verde and is fairly common within the saguaro's range. It is named for the feathery pink blooms which appear in the spring and summer. Brittlebush is a grayish-green plant whose large, yellow flowers often color the hillsides in the spring. Two or three feet tall, this is one of the area's largest and most common members of the sunflower family, of which there are many. The stems of the brittlebush exude a gummy material which was chewed by the Indians. It was also used as an incense in the early churches of the area, thus the Spanish name, "encienso."

The mesquite tree is a very common plant along river courses and arroyos.

The ocotillo loses its leaves during dry periods, but is covered with dark green foliage during the rainy season. The tree growing by the saguaro is a palo verde. (Photo by E. Driscoll-Hunt.)

Many different species of cacti live in close association with the saguaro. One of the most noticeable of these is Engelmann's prickly pear, a plant with large, flat stems. These plants often sprawl over a large area, providing shelter for numerous creatures beneath their prickly pad-like stems. Ground squirrels dig their burrows beneath them. Packrats pile sticks, stones, and cholla joints within their midst, providing formidable fortress against intruders. Diamondback rattlesnakes are often found coiled in the shade beneath large prickly pear plants.

The dark red fruit of this cactus, which ripens in the late summer, is eaten by many different animals. Wasps, beetles, squirrels, tortoises, and birds are among the smaller species. Javelinas, skunks and other animals also enjoy the delicious fruit.

There are a number of species of cholla cacti growing within the saguaro community. One of the most common is the jumping cholla, so named because of its loosely attached stem joints which so easily stick to the passer-by that they seemingly jump upon him. This cactus is armed with many sharp, minutely-barbed spines. It is a favorite nesting site for both the cactus wren and the curve-billed thrasher. Roadrunners, doves, house finches, and other birds nest in it as well.

Even more densely-spined is the teddy bear cholla. At a distance this cactus takes on a soft, yellowish appearance, much like a teddy bear, but close inspection soon proves this to be quite the opposite. It, too, is used as a nesting site by many birds.

The barrel cactus is a large plant which is sometimes mistaken for a small saguaro, but is easily distinguished from it by the presense of heavy, curved spines. The barrel cactus blooms much later in the year than most of the cacti, the flowers appearing in the late summer. Since many of the barrel cacti lean toward the south, this cactus is often called "compass cactus."

The jumping cholla is a very common plant in the saguaro community. Because of its formidable spines, many birds use it for a nesting site.

The teddybear cholla is a heavily-spined plant which prefers rocky outcroppings. Notice the cactus wren's nest at the top of the plant.

Sometimes the barrel cactus is mistaken for a young saguaro, but it is much more robust and has long, recurved spines.

The smallest and least noticeable of the cacti is the pincushion cactus. Only a few inches high, this little plant usually grows beneath the protective shelter of a palo verde, cholla, bursage, or other larger plant. In the summer its top is ringed by pink flowers, followed by bright red fruit.

Probably the most numerous plant of the saguaro community is the bursage, a small relative of the ragweed. Scarcely over a foot in height, it is closely spaced across the desert floor, providing cover for many small creatures as they travel back and forth, and for many smaller plants as well, including seedling saguaros. Bursage plants also aid greatly in holding the soil together, preventing erosion by wind and rain. During dry seasons its leaves wither and turn dark, but when rain is plentiful it grows soft, green leaves. Some of the small, pale flowers of the bursage produce pollen which often causes allergic reactions among the hay fever sufferers of the area.

There are hundreds of other plants, both large and small, which live in close association with the saguaro. Some are large cacti such as the organ pipe and senita, which are closely related to the giant cactus. Some like the ironwood and creosote bush are large trees or shrubs.

Many of the desert plants are small and only appear upon occasion, springing forth from seeds which may have lain dormant for several years, germinating only when the climatic conditions are just right. These are among the most colorful, for they bear flowers of many different hues. There are many grasses also, often dry and brown, but with a good rainy season these become green and luxuriant.

All of these plants provide food for many wild creatures, and when they are plentiful, populations of the animals which feed upon them may also rise. Food, shelter, oxygen-production and erosion control—without the plants, other life could not exist.

The saguaro community—In the foreground are the small bursages, Engelmann's prickly pear is scattered about, the tree to the far right is an ironwood, the one on the far left is a palo verde. Several species of cholla cactus are also present.

Chapter 7

Man's Relationship to the Saguaro and Other Large Cacti

For centuries, the Papago Indian tribe has harvested the ripe fruit of the saguaro cactus. As soon as the first fruit began to split open, revealing red interiors, the Papagos would travel into the saguaro forest and set up their seasonal camps. Their shelters usually consisted of open ramadas, constructed of mesquite poles and covered with whatever material was available. Early each morning they would walk out into the desert, carrying with them woven baskets. At a fair distance from the campsite, they would turn about and head back again, putting the ripe fruit into their baskets as they returned. In this manner, the baskets would be filled by the time they arrived back in camp.

The tool used to knock the ripe fruit from the top of the saguaro's stem and arms was called a "kuibit". This was a long pole made by tying two or more saguaro ribs together. At one end and again about one-third of the way down were tied short pieces of the rib, crossing the kuibit at forty-five degree angles. These were the prongs used to knock or pull the fruit from the saguaro.

When the Indians returned to camp, they would dump their loads of fruit into a container—usually an earthen pot—filled with water. The fruit was allowed to soak for a time with occasional stirrings and skimmings of the surface to remove any foreign substances. The pot was then put upon an open fire to boil.

After boiling for a short time, the pot was removed from the fire and the contents strained through a loosely woven basket. The pulp and seeds removed in this manner were spread out in the sun to dry. The dried pulp and seed mixture was used for many purposes. It could be eaten just as it was, or it could be mixed with other edible materials. Some of it was stored in vessels for later use in the jam-making process. Many of the seeds were removed, roasted and sweetened to make candy, or ground into a meal and made into a gravy.

The juice was once again put upon the fire to boil. In the meantime, some of the stored pulp and seed mixture was soaked in water and most of the seeds removed by dipping portions of it in and out of pots of water, using a heavily-spined section of ocotillo as a dipping tool. The pulp would stick to the spines, the seeds remaining in the water. The pulp was then dropped into another container. When the boiling of the juice was at the right stages, this pulp was added and the boiling continued, until a thick jam resulted. The jam was sealed in containers for future use.

Near the end of the saguaro harvest season, the Papagos would store some of the saguaro juice, allowing it to ferment into a wine called "tiswin." This was used in their rain-making ceremonies, but not before the fruit was harvested, for they did not want the storms to begin early, knocking off the ripened fruit and drenching their camp.

A Papago Indian woman picks saguaro fruit, using the lower prong of the harvest pole.

Cooking saguaro fruit in a Papago Indian harvest camp.

This same process of saguaro harvest and jam-making continues today. Now, however, the Indians arrive at the camps in automobiles or pickup trucks, carrying their water in steel drums or aluminum beer kegs. The black kettle has replaced the earthen pot, and screen wire is used instead of a woven basket to strain the pulp. But the rest of the procedure is pretty much the same as it was centuries ago. The wooden-pole ramadas are still used, and so are the kuibits, many of them having been carefully retained for years.

There are several other large cacti commonly occurring within the saguaro's range which have also been of economic importance to the natives of the region. The most notable of these are the organ pipe, senita, and cardon. Two of these—the organ pipe and senita—occur in a small area of southwestern Arizona. All three are common along the western coast of Sonora and on many of the islands of the Gulf of California.

The organ pipe cactus branches from a central stem at ground level, its many long stems resembling the pipe organ for which it is named. These stems may often reach the height of twenty feet or more. The flowers are somewhat similar in shape and size to those of the saguaro, and are of a pale pink hue. They open at night and close much earlier in the morning than do the saguaro flowers. The fruit are red and spiny.

The organ pipe cactus is a close relative of the saguaro.

The senita, closely related to the organ pipe and saguaro, occurs in southwestern Arizona and northwestern Mexico.

The senita cactus somewhat resembles an organ pipe cactus, but the stem has fewer ribs and fewer spines along most of its surface. It is also called the "old man cactus" because of the thick growth of bristly, whisker-like spines which grow from the upper portion of the older stems. Like the organ pipe, the senita branches from the base into many arms and may reach a height of over twenty feet but is usually not that tall. It bears small, night-blooming flowers of pinkish coloration.

The cardon, or sahueso, resembles the saguaro in general appearance but is larger. Its trunk and arms are greater in diameter than those of the saguaro, and it often possesses more arms. Sometimes reaching a height of over 50 feet, the cardon is the world's largest cactus. Its flowers are similar to those of the saguaro, but more yellow in coloration. The outside of the cardon's fruit is very spiny.

Whereas the fruit-gathering activities of the Papago Indians center mainly in the saguaro forests of southern Arizona, those of the Seri Indians of Mexico take place along the western coast of Sonora, and on many of the Gulf of California islands. The Seri have long made use of the large, columnar cacti, not only as a food item, but for building, medicine, games, religion and many other purposes.

The ribs of these large cacti were used as toys and in games. Saguaro fruit skins were used as targets for sharp pointed sticks in one game, while in another, chunks of cactus flesh, the spines removed, were thrown at opponents. A section of senita stem was fashioned into a child's toy somewhat resembling a dumbbell, while the "boot" or "shoe" which once was a bird's nesting cavity in a saguaro or cardon was used to carry a little girl's doll.

Chunks of saguaro or cardon were heated in coals, wrapped in cloths, and placed on an aching body. Cardon juice mixed with charcoal was used for tattooing. The oil from mashed organ pipe seeds was used to soften deer skins, while the dried inner portion of the plant was ground into a powder, mixed with animal fat, and heated over a fire to produce a pitch for caulking the seams of the Seri's wooden boats.

Occurring within the saguaro's range along the northern coast of the Gulf of California,
the cardon is the world's largest cactus.

The wooden skeleton of a saguaro still stands among its living relatives. Bursage, ocotillo, jumping cholla, palo verde and prickly pear can also be seen in this photo. The bush in the left center is a jojoba, the seeds of which produce a highly sought after oil.

The large columnar cacti have also played an important role in the religion of the Seri Indians, these plants being thought to contain strong spirits. A fire was made at the base of a saguaro to stop rain. The wind was calmed by slicing an organ pipe stem into eight pieces and throwing them into the sea, one at a time. By cutting a hole in a senita stem and placing a lock of human's hair in it, a curse could be placed upon that person. In legend, in religion, and in practical use, the saguaro and other large cacti have played an important role in the lives of the Seri Indians.

The Indians are not the only people who make use of the saguaro. The living plant is much in demand for landscaping in Arizona yards and gardens, and nurseries sell them for high prices. It is illegal to go into the desert to dig up one's own. Anyone doing so without a permit faces a severe fine.

Saguaro ribs from a dead plant, or even an entire skeleton, are often used for decoration or building purposes. Fences and screenings have been constructed of ribs, but the task is time consuming and not many attempt it. This is fortunate, for the dead skeleton, whether standing upright, as often is the case, or lying outstretched upon the desert floor, provides shelter for many small creatures, and eventually returns to the soil. Cutting up dead saguaros and hauling them into one's yard for building purposes destroys the habitat of many things. The great importance of a dead saguaro to its environment will be further discussed in the next chapter.

Unfortunately, man's relationship to the saguaro is not only that of food harvester, decorator, or builder, but many times also that of destroyer. The rapid spread of housing developments continues to take a great toll of these giant cacti, as do highways which cut through the saguaro forests. But developers alone are not at fault for the destruction of the saguaro; many specimens succumb to the careless and thoughtless acts of individual persons.

Although all saguaros are protected by State law, in some areas—such as the Saguaro National Monument and the Organ Pipe Cactus National Monument—they are closely and actively protected by Park Service personnel. In places such as these, mankind is doing its best to keep the giant cactus alive and well. In spite of all efforts, there are some areas where the saguaro numbers are decreasing. This is not necessarily due to changes brought about by humans, but may be caused by changes in climate or other natural causes. In some areas, saguaro populations are actually increasing. Research into these changes is another part of man's relationship to the saguaro. Scientists at educational and research institutions are carefully studying the factors involved with the rise and fall of saguaro populations. In the meantime, we as individuals should be sure to do what we can to prevent the destruction of this unique and fascinating plant.

This photograph, taken from the main patio of the Arizona-Sonora Desert Museum in 1952 shows at least 30 large saguaros in plain view. Compare this with the photo below.

This photo, taken from the same location in 1980, shows that at least two-thirds of the large plants have succumbed. (The seven foot specimen on the left was planted.) Compare the length of the arms on the cacti in this photo to those on the photo above to get an idea of arm-growth rate.

Chapter 8

Death of
a Saguaro

A number of circumstances may lead to a saguaro's death. During an unusual cold spell the temperature may drop below freezing for 24 hours or more and tissue destruction results. Usually it is only the smaller plants which die immediately, the larger specimens suffering damaged tissues which may later cause the saguaro's death through bacterial infection or other causes. This condition is rare, occurring only in limited areas at the higher elevations of the saguaro's northern range.

During the summer, sudden strong winds may uproot a large saguaro, particularly if the soil around its roots has been dampened by heavy rainfall, or disturbed by construction. Recent studies show that many saguaro falls are due to root structures weakened by a fungus. An otherwise healthy plant blown over by the wind often lies upon the ground for weeks or even months before decaying, particularly if some of the root structure is still embedded in the ground.

A blizzard blows through saguaro-land. This is
a rare occurrence, and such a storm may
not take place more than once every several years.

Bacterial infection near the base of this large cactus has weakened it and it has toppled. Soon the tissues will decay and nothing will be left but ribs. During this time, however, the fallen giant will provide much food and shelter for a myriad of creatures.

Although not a common occurrence, lightning will strike a saguaro. Here, death and decay are immediate, for the tissues are badly damaged by the electrical current passing through them and within a few days the large cactus begins to rot and fall apart. On occasion a saguaro will literally explode when struck, due to the high pressure caused when the water in its cells turns to steam. No doubt a few saguaros are struck during each severe thunderstorm which passes through their area.

Vandalism is also a cause of death of the saguaro. The trunks of saguaros are hacked with machetes, and initials are carved into their sides with knives. Sticks and stones are often found deeply embedded in their sides, and many have been riddled with bullets or pierced with arrows during some thoughtless person's target practice. Such injuries may result in the infection and death of the plant, and within a very short time a cactus that took decades to grow is gone. Not only is the plant gone, but also the seeds which it would have produced, and the food and shelter it could have provided, perhaps for many more decades to come.

The spread of modern civilization also takes its toll of saguaros. Vast areas of desert land are bulldozed to build housing developments, shopping centers, and other commercial ventures. Mine dumps sprawl across the landscape, burying plants beneath them. Pipelines, powerlines, and highways cut wide swaths through miles of prime saguaro habitat.

Lightning storms are frequent and intense in the
desert, and saguaros sometimes fall
victim to direct strikes.

This saguaro—located at a viewing stop
on Saguaro National Monument's loop road,
has suffered from many thrown sticks and stones.

The individual organism which perhaps most often causes a saguaro's death is the bacterium known to scientists as *Erwinia carnegieana*. Once this bacterium enters the tissues of the giant cactus it quickly breaks down the cells. Large black masses of decayed tissue result, sometimes in the form of a thick, black liquid which oozes from the saguaro's side. The infection can spread rapidly, and within a few weeks the entire structure is weakened and begins to collapse. The top of the stem and the arms may break off and fall to the ground, and soon nothing is left but the lower skeleton, partially covered by the hollow outer layer of its bark-like tissues.

A saguaro standing near an infected one may actually have the disease transmitted to it through the root system, but those farther away are also in danger, for the *Cactobrosis* moth has been proven to be the prime carrier of *Erwinia*. The moth larvae hatch from eggs laid on the side of the plant and burrow their way into the tissues. The bacteria, which have been carried from moth to egg to larvae, then attack the tissues and the disease has begun. Many times the saguaro is able to build up a protection of corky material around the infection, sealing it off from the rest of the plant, much in the same manner as it seals off the nest cavities dug by the woodpeckers. These small, hardened masses can be found in the debris of any dead saguaro.

Experiments have been conducted by injecting antibiotics into the affected areas. If only localized in a very small area, the treatment may work, otherwise it does not. Needless to say, it would be an impossible task to locate and treat all of the plants infected with *Erwinia*. Like freezing, being blown over by the wind, or struck by lightning, the bacterium is a natural cause of death. Some saguaros will die from this cause, others will not.

Whatever the cause of death may be, a dead or dying saguaro is still a vital part of its community. The tissue begins to decay, which is the action of many organisms feeding upon the dead tissues. Numerous small creatures come to feed upon it. The larvae of certain types of flies and beetles, for example, depend upon this source of food for their existence. Larvae of other insects in turn feed upon them. The soft, oozing mass which is the interior of a dying saguaro literally teems with life of this sort.

As the soft tissues are broken down by the numerous organisms feeding upon them, the ribs and harder layers of tissues are left, and it is among these that a great variety of wildlife exists. In a dead saguaro which is still standing erect, black-widow spiders spin their webs, giant crab spiders hunt for insects, and desert spiny lizards and others hide beneath the outer covering. Banded geckos, small snakes, and cactus mice find shelter within the root structures, particularly during the winter months.

The gecko is a tiny lizard which hides among the debris of fallen saguaros. At night it fallen saguaros. At night it emerges to feed on insects.

The black widow—easily distinquished by the red hour glass on her tummy—is a very common spider in saguaro country. Although possessing a very toxic venom, few fatalities occur, due to the spider's retiring disposition.

A stripe-tailed scorpion—one of several species found in the saguaro community. The sting of this three-inch long creature is no more severe than that of a bee.

In saguaros fallen to the ground, an even greater variety of life may be found. Scorpions, spiders and centipedes dwell beneath the debris, not only using it for shelter, but also as a hunting ground for the many insects and other small animals living there. Pinacate beetles, cactus beetles, millipedes and many other creatures which feed upon nearby plants find refuge from daytime heat beneath the dead saguaro carcass, coming out to feed during the cooler morning and evening hours. Animals as large as a six-foot gopher snake, or as small as the tiny, pinhead-sized pseudoscorpion may be found within the debris of a fallen saguaro.

Slowly the saguaro returns to the desert soil from which it came. In its final stages, termites cover its wooden ribs with their mud tunnels, beneath which they chew steadily away, gradually reducing the wooden fibers to usable food material with the aid of the microbes which dwell within their intestines. Within the remnants of callous tissue and ribs, a seedling palo verde pushes its way upwards. Perhaps eventually it will serve as nurse plant for a young saguaro, and during future decades a giant will again dominate the landscape where the fallen one stood.

The Arizona coral snake is ringed with alternating black, white, and red bands. Although the venom is highly toxic, this snake only reaches a length of approximately 22 inches and there are no recorded fatalities from this species.